ALL
ABOUT
MYTHS

CHINESE
MYTHS AND
LEGENDS

Anita Ganeri

Raintree
Chicago, Illinois

Edited by Nancy Dickmann and Abby Colich
Designed by Jo Hinton-Malivoire
Original illustrations © Capstone Global Library
    Ltd 2013
Illustrations by Xöul
Picture research by Elizabeth Alexander
Production by Victoria Fitzgerald
Originated by Capstone Global Library Ltd
Printed and bound in China by China Translation
    and Printing Services

17 16 15 14 13
10 9 8 7 6 5 4 3 2 1

**Library of Congress Cataloging-in-
Publication Data**
Ganeri, Anita, 1961-
  Chinese myths and legends / Anita Ganeri.—1
[edition].
    p. cm.—(All about myths)
  Includes bibliographical references and index.
  ISBN 978-1-4109-5467-1 (hb)—ISBN 978-1-4109-
5473-2 (pb) 1. Mythology, Chinese—Juvenile
literature. I. Title.

  BL1825.G35 2013
  398.20931—dc23   2012043969

Acknowledgments
We would like to thank the following for
permission to reproduce photographs:
Alamy: pp. 12 (© Danita Delimont), 14 (© Iain
Masterton), 15 (© David Lyons), 16 (© Mary
Evans Picture Library), 20 (© B Christopher), 21
(© Lordprice Collection), 22 (© Louise Batalla
Duran), 28 (© Ivy Close Images), 29 (© Louise
Batalla Duran), 37 (© GL Archive); Art Archive:
p. 40 (Victoria and Albert Museum London /
Eileen Tweedy); Corbis: p. 17 (© Heritage Images);
Getty Images: pp. 7 (Keren Su /China Span),
11 (Dorling Kindersley), 13 (China Photos), 23
(Chinese School/The Bridgeman Art Library),
25 (DeAgostini/G. DAGLI ORTI), 36 (Dorling
Kindersley); public domain: p. 10 (c.Lions Gate/Everett); Shutterstock: pp. 4-5 (©
Hung Chung Chih), 6 (© iBird), 24 (© jejim), 30 (©
panda3800), 31 (© i4lcocl2); The Bridgeman Art
Library: pp. 34 (Giraudon), 35 (© FuZhai Archive).

Design features: Shutterstock (© Vangelis76, ©
chuyu, © Repina Valeriya, © Ptahi, © Kongsak, ©
Pan Xunbin, © Regien Paassen, © jomphong, ©
sainum).

Cover photograph of a carved stone statue of
the Buddhist Goddess Kuan Yin reproduced with
permission from Superstock (© Ron Chapple
Photography / SuperFusion). Background image
reproduced with permission from Shutterstock (©
Martin Capek).

The publishers would like to thank Seth Wiener for
his invaluable help in the preparation of this book.

Every effort has been made to contact copyright
holders of any material reproduced in this book.
Any omissions will be rectified in subsequent
printings if notice is given to the publisher.

Disclaimer
All the Internet addresses (URLs) given in this
book were valid at the time of going to press.
However, due to the dynamic nature of the
Internet, some addresses may have changed,
or sites may have changed or ceased to exist
since publication. While the author and publisher
regret any inconvenience this may cause readers,
no responsibility for any such changes can be
accepted by either the author or the publisher.

CONTENTS

Did you know?

Discover some interesting facts about Chinese myths.

WHO'S WHO?

Find out more about some of the main characters in Chinese myths.

MYTH LINKS

Learn about similar characters or stories from other cultures.

ANCIENT CHINA

China is one of the world's most ancient civilizations, dating back to about 5,000 BCE. From around 1766 BCE, China was ruled by the Shang dynasty, then by the Zhou. As Zhou rule weakened, China broke up into many small states that were constantly at war. In 221 BCE, the state of Qin took control. The Qin ruler, Qin Shi Huang, became the first emperor of China and united the country for the first time. The system of government he set in place stayed almost unchanged for the next 2,000 years.

Did you know?

Chinese myths were probably first passed on by word of mouth. Later, they were written down in a huge number of ancient texts. For example, the stories of Yu (see page 12) and many other mythical figures are told in the *Classic of the Mountains and the Seas*, which dates from around the 3rd century BCE.

The Great Wall of China snakes for thousands of miles across China. Parts of the wall date from the reign of Emperor Qin Shi Huang.

MYTHS AND LEGENDS

Myths and legends are traditional stories. Most are not based in historical fact, but tell stories about gods and goddesses, supernatural beings, and events, such as the creation of the world and what happens after death. People have been telling these stories since ancient times to help make sense of their lives and the world around them.

The ancient Chinese had a vast collection of myths. Many of them told stories of the gods, goddesses, and immortals, or tried to explain events, such as how the world was made. These myths came mainly from China's three religions: Confucianism, Taoism, and Buddhism. Many myths contained a mixture of elements from all three religions.

CREATION AND DESTRUCTION

In Chinese mythology, the universe was a vast, square piece of land, surrounded by four seas: the East Sea, West Sea, South Sea, and North Sea. The four corners of the land were held up by a giant tortoise's feet (see page 35). Above the land was the sky, which was divided into nine parts and had nine layers. In the ninth, and topmost, layer lived the Jade Emperor.

HEAVENLY LINKS

There were many links between heaven and Earth that were used by the gods and goddesses. The main sky ladder was a huge tree, called Jian Mu, located in Duguang, a mythical paradise on Earth. The tree had been planted by the Yellow Emperor. It had no branches but a towering trunk, dark green leaves, and black flowers.

MYTH LINKS

In Norse mythology, a gigantic tree, called Yggdrasill, stood at the center of the universe. It was so vast that it held the whole world in place and shaded it with its branches. Many creatures lived on Yggdrasill, including a dragon, called Nidhogg, who gnawed constantly at its roots.

This traditional ink and wash painting shows a Chinese landscape.

Another sky ladder was the sacred mountain, Mount Kunlun (above). It was the home of the gods and goddesses on Earth, where they lived in 12 splendid palaces, built on a huge rock on the mountaintop. The mountain was guarded by Lu Wu, a god with a human

Pan Gu Creates the World

For thousands of years, the god Pan Gu lay in a deep sleep, gathering the strength he would need to create the world. Finally, one day, Pan Gu woke up and looked about. All around him lay darkness and chaos. Pan Gu was not pleased—this was not the world he had hoped to find. He lashed out in anger, smashing his gigantic fist into the chaos with an almighty booming sound.

Pan Gu's blow sent the universe reeling, but then, the chaos began to settle down and order took its place. The heavy things sank down to form the rocks of Earth, while the lighter things floated upward to form the sky.

Day by day, the Earth and sky kept on growing, thicker, deeper, and higher. Fearful that they would collapse, Pan Gu stood between them, using all of his great strength to hold them apart. As the Earth and sky grew, so did Pan Gu, pushing them further and further apart. When he was sure that they were fixed in place, he lay down again and fell, exhausted, into a deep sleep.

Pan Gu never woke up again. As he slept, he died, and the different parts of his body formed the world. His breath formed the wind and clouds; his voice rumbled as thunder. His eyes became the sun and moon, and the hair of his beard became the stars. Great mountains formed from Pan Gu's vast body; his arms and legs became the four points of the compass. His blood flowed out and filled the rivers; his flesh turned into the soil in the fields. Then the hairs on his head took root in the soil and sprouted into trees and flowers. Pan Gu's sweat turned into rain to water them and formed the morning dew.

And so, Pan Gu created the world out of darkness and chaos.

THE FIRST PEOPLE

The goddess Nü Wa liked to visit Pan Gu's new world but, despite its beauty, she found it empty and lonely. Picking up a lump of soft, yellowish clay from the ground, she began to mold it into a figure with a head, body, arms, and legs.

When she placed the figure on the ground, it came to life—the first human. Nü Wa was delighted and began to make more figures. When she got tired, she mixed the clay with water, dipped a piece of rope in it, then flicked the rope so that drops of clay landed everywhere. Each drop became a new person.

WHO'S WHO?

Nü Wa (above) was a goddess of creation and marriage. In many paintings and images, she is shown with the head of a woman but the body of a snake or dragon. In some stories, she is said to be the wife of the god Fu Xi (see page 37). In others, she is his sister.

SOLVING THE PROBLEM

At first, the people seemed happy, but, after a while, they began to grow old. Nü Wa realized that they would die soon. So she gave them the ability to get married and have children. That way there would always be humans to live on Earth.

MYTH LINKS

Many cultures have myths about the creation of humans. In the myth of the Yoruba people of West Africa, the god Obatala climbs down from heaven on a gold chain. He creates the land but feels lonely, so he digs up some clay and molds it into the first people. Then the sky god, Olorun, breathes life into the figures.

■ Obatala of West African Yoruba mythology is shown here.

NATURAL DISASTERS

Many Chinese myths tell of natural disasters in which the gods come to the help of humans. Once, there were 10 suns in the sky, and they took it in turns to shine. This way, Earth was warm enough for crops to grow and everyone was happy. Then, one day, all 10 suns decided to shine at the same time. In the scorching heat, the crops died and people began to starve. The Jade Emperor called on his finest archer, Hou Yi. One by one, Hou Yi shot down the suns, until only one remained and Earth was saved.

GUN SAVES EARTH

Long ago, the Yellow Emperor sent a terrible flood to punish humans for their wicked ways. Rivers burst their banks, houses and crops were washed away, and people drowned. Gun, the Emperor's grandson, took pity on the people. He took some soil from heaven and spread it on Earth to soak up the water. His grandfather was furious. He sent more rain down and ordered Gun to be killed. But, instead of blood, a young dragon emerged from Gun's body. The dragon was Gun's son, Yu, who was finally able to stop the flood.

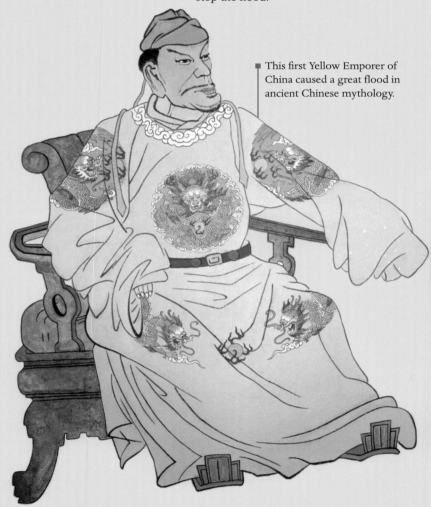

■ This first Yellow Emporer of China caused a great flood in ancient Chinese mythology.

Did you know?

Millions of people live along the banks of China's two great rivers: the Yellow and the Yangtze. They rely on the rivers for transportation, food, and water. Over the centuries, the rivers have flooded many times with devastating results. Thousands of people have died in floods, and millions have been forced to leave their homes.

GODS AND IMMORTALS

Three great religions were followed in ancient China: Confucianism, Taoism, and Buddhism. Over the centuries, their beliefs and myths mixed together, producing a huge collection of stories.

CONFUCIANISM

The great philosopher Confucius was a real person born in 551 BCE, at a time of social unrest in China. He dedicated his life to finding a better way for people to live and behave. At the heart of his teaching were family values and respect for other people, along with the five virtues of kindness, righteousness, sobriety, wisdom, and trustworthiness.

Did you know?

Confucius (right) was famous for his wise sayings, which summed up his teachings. Two examples are: "A good person always seeks to help others to do good, not to do ill." And, "When you say something, say what you know. When you don't know something, say you don't know. That is knowledge."

Did you know?

According to Taoism, everything in the world is made up of two forces, called yin and yang. In nature, they are carefully balanced. If things go wrong, for example if someone falls ill, it is because the natural balance has been upset.

TAOISM

Taoism was founded in the 6th century BCE by the philosopher Laozi. Legend says that he left his job and rode off on the back of an ox to the mountains, where he wrote down his teachings. Laozi taught people that the way to achieve everlasting life was to follow the Tao, or "Way." This was a spiritual force that existed in everything in the universe. Following the Tao meant leading a simple, good life in harmony with nature and the world around you.

A statue showing Laozi setting off on an ox into the mountains.

GODS AND GODDESSES

Ancient Chinese myths include stories about a huge number of gods and goddesses who affected Chinese life in many ways. Some had set roles, for example as guardians of rivers or gods of marriage. Others protected people and could be called on in times of need.

THE HEAVENLY COURT

In many ways, the lives of the Chinese gods and goddesses mirrored life on Earth. Heaven had its own emperor, called the Jade Emperor, who lived in a magnificent palace, surrounded by hundreds of servants. On Earth, the real Chinese emperor had a huge civil service of ministers to help him govern the country. In heaven, the gods and goddesses were organized in a similar way. They were divided into different departments that helped the Jade Emperor to rule. The gods also acted as messengers between heaven and Earth. The only human to whom the Jade Emperor spoke directly was the earthly emperor himself.

In Chinese mythology, the Jade Emperor (right) is the ruler of Heaven, Earth, and Hell.

WHO'S WHO?

Queen Xi Wangmu was the second most important figure in the heavenly court. She was also known as the Queen Mother of the West. She lived on Mount Kunlun and had the power to grant everlasting life, by offering people a special elixir or one of the peaches of immortality that she grew in her garden.

MYTH LINKS

In ancient Greek mythology, the all-powerful king of the gods is Zeus. God of the sky and thunder, he rules over the other gods and goddesses in their home on Mount Olympus in Greece. His wife was the goddess Hera, who was famous for her beauty.

The Goddess in the Moon

The beautiful goddess Chang E lived in heaven with her husband, Hou Yi, the archer. Their lives were happy and carefree until Hou Yi shot down the nine suns. Their father, Dun Ji, was so grief-stricken that he banished them to live on Earth as mortals, not as gods.

One day, Hou Yi visited the home of Xi Wangmu, the Queen Mother of the West, where he built her a magnificent palace of jade. In return, she gave Hou Yi a bottle of the elixir of immortality and, with it, his chance to return to heaven. But there was a catch...

"Be warned," Queen Xi Wangmu told him. "There is enough elixir for two. But if one person drinks it all, they will leave the world and never return."

Heeding her words, Hou Yi wrapped the bottle in silk and hid it carefully in the roof of his house, but not carefully enough! One day, while Hou Yi was out, Chang E noticed a strange glowing light coming from the roof and climbed up to find out where it was coming from. There she found the bottle, shining brightly through the silk. Chang E could not resist, despite the warning. She opened the bottle and drank the elixir straight down.

Immediately, the elixir began to take effect. Chang E floated up to the ceiling, then out of the door. She was helpless to do anything about it. Higher and higher she floated, until she reached the moon. She has stayed there ever since, with only a hare for company.

When Hou Yi discovered what foolish Chang E had done, he was filled with dismay. He had lost both his wife and his chance for immortality. But the gods took pity on him. They allowed him to return to heaven. And, at the time of the full moon, he is allowed to visit Chang E in her palace on the moon.

THE EIGHT IMMORTALS

The eight immortals were eight mythological figures, worshipped by Taoists. They later became hugely popular in Chinese culture generally. They had started off as mortals on Earth, but achieved immortality by their devotion to the Tao. They were said to live on a remote group of islands and to have magical powers, such as becoming invisible, healing the sick, or turning objects into gold.

ZHONGLI QUAN

The leader of the immortals, Zhongli Quan, spent his life working as an officer at the emperor's court, but became a holy man in his old age. One day, as he sat meditating in a cave, great cracks appeared and split the walls apart. A new cave appeared that glowed with a strange light. Inside, Zhongli Quan found a casket made of the finest jade, which opened and revealed to him the secrets of immortality.

Li Tieguai became immortal after studying for many years with Laozi himself.

This illustration shows the eight immortals crossing the sea.

WHO'S WHO?

The eight immortals:

- Li Tieguai: walks with an iron crutch; gives out special medicine from a gourd
- Zhongli Quan: owns a magic fan that can bring the dead back to life
- Lü Dongbin: scholarly and clever; turned to Taoism after a dream
- Cao Guojiu: gave up his high position at court and his wealth to follow the Tao
- He Xiangu: the only female immortal; holds a life-giving lotus flower
- Han Xiang Zi: follower of Lü Dongbin; has a magic flute that gives life
- Zhang Guo Lao: hermit who knew magic; owned a magic mule that could be folded up
- Lan Caihe: famous healer; shown as a man or a woman

CAO GUOJIU

Cao Guojiu was said to be the brother of a real empress and had an important position at court. But he decided to give away all of his money and went into the mountains to live as a holy man. He kept one reminder of his past: a tablet made from gold, which showed that he was a courtier.

One day, he wanted to cross the river but did not have any money to pay the ferryman. Instead, he showed him the tablet to get a free passage. The ferryman did not like his boasting and refused to take him. So Cao Guojiu threw the tablet into the water as a sign that his old life was truly over. The ferryman, who was actually Lü Dongbin (see below), was so impressed that he took Cao Guojiu on as his pupil and taught him the Tao.

Lü Dongbin was a clever scholar who became Cao Guojiu's teacher.

LÜ DONGBIN

Lü Dongbin turned to Taoism after a dream. He dreamt that he had a good job at court and for many years did well and grew very rich. Then, one day, he was ~~stripped of his honors and had a ...~~ court. His dream showed him that worldly success could end in disaster, and he decided to study the Tao. As an immortal, he is shown dressed as a scholar, carrying a sword that could make him invisible.

WHO'S WHO?

He Xiangu (left) was the only female immortal. As a young girl, she had a dream telling her to go to the Mother of Pearl mountains, where she would become immortal. She is sometimes shown holding a lotus flower and a musical instrument, called a sheng.

BUDDHIST MYTHS

The third great religion of China, Buddhism, began in India around the 5th century BCE, and is based on the teachings of an Indian nobleman named Siddhartha Gautama. He gave up his life of luxury to live as a wandering holy man and seek the truth about how to live a good, happy life. When he finally became enlightened, he was given the title of the Buddha (awakened one).

Buddhism reached China in around the 1st century CE. It was probably spread by merchants traveling from India through Central Asia along the Silk Road. Buddhism developed alongside Confucianism and Taoism, becoming China's third religion. By the 4th century CE, there were 24,000 Buddhist monks in China, and almost 2,000 monasteries.

This Buddhist pagoda is located in Baodingshan, Dazu, China.

PURE LAND BUDDHISM

One of the most important figures in Chinese Buddhism is Amituo Fu. He began life as a monk named Dharmakara, and gained enlightenment through his good deeds. He is said to live in a heavenly place called the Pure Land.

By having faith in Amituo Fu and chanting his name, people believe that they will be reborn in the Pure Land.

Did you know?

To collect Buddhist texts for translation, Chinese monks made long, daring journeys to India. Faxian (338–422 CE) set off in 399. He finally reached India after crossing the deadly Taklamakan Desert and the Pamir Mountains. At the time, people believed that the mountains were home to terrifying dragons that spat out poison.

Monkey and the Heavenly Peaches

Long ago, a stone monkey hatched out of a stone egg. The monkey was clever and brave, and quickly became the Monkey King. Not content, he wanted to become immortal and begged the gods to tell him how. When they refused, he stole the book of judgments and crossed out his name and the age at which he would die.

The gods were furious. They went to the Jade Emperor to complain.

"We're fed up with his mischief," they said. "Something has got to be done."

The Jade Emperor decided to give the Monkey King a job to keep him out of trouble. He made him Keeper of the Heavenly Peach Garden, where the peaches of immortality grew. Monkey couldn't believe his luck!

All went well until the gods held their yearly peach banquet and forgot to invite the Monkey King. Furious, he crept into the garden, picked all the peaches, and gobbled them down. He was immortal at last! The Jade Emperor sent his army to capture him but, by that time, he had run far away.

In despair, the gods called on the Buddha. The Buddha gave the Monkey King a test.

"If you can jump out of my hand and across the world," he said, "you will become ruler of Heaven and take the Jade Emperor's place."

"No problem," replied the Monkey King, and took a gigantic leap. He jumped right across the heavens, landing at the foot of a tall mountain. Then he bounded back to the Buddha's palm. The Buddha said nothing but pointed to his hand. The mountain was no further than the tip of one of the Buddha's fingers.

The Monkey King was defeated. As punishment, he was locked inside a magic mountain until he was truly sorry for all the wrongs he had done, and the kindly Buddha set him free again.

THE UNDERWORLD

Buddhists believe that when a person dies, they are reborn in a different form, which can be a human, animal, or plant. Good actions in this life lead to a good rebirth. In Chinese Buddhism, the souls of the dead travel to the Underworld to be judged. This is a terrible place, with a series of courts handing out dreadful punishments to those who have led wicked lives. At the final court, a decision is made about what a person's next life will be like.

MULIAN'S MOTHER

There was once a monk, Mulian, who left his mother money to give to the monks who came to her door. But his mother kept the money for herself and lied to Mulian. She was sent to hell, where she became a ghost that was always hungry but had a neck so thin that she could not swallow any food.

MYTH LINKS

In Greek mythology, the hero Orpheus journeys to the Underworld to find his dead wife, Eurydice (both shown left). God of the Underworld, Hades, allows Orpheus to lead Eurydice back to the land of the living as long as he does not look at her. But Orpheus cannot resist a glimpse, so Hades snatches Eurydice back.

The Festival of the Hungry Ghosts is celebrated each year in China. This is when the gates of hell are opened and the hungry ghosts are free to wander Earth. People leave out offerings of food on the streets, in homes, and in Buddhist temples.

DRAGONS AND MYTHICAL CREATURES

Dragons are an important part of Chinese mythology. In Western legends, dragons were usually fearsome, fire-breathing beasts. Chinese dragons were extremely powerful, but also kind and wise. They were worshipped as rulers of nature and bringers of water and rain.

They symbolized good luck, wealth, and justice. Dragons were also the symbols of the Chinese emperor. As a sign of their royal power, emperors' robes and palaces were often decorated with images of dragons.

Chinese dragons were usually long, scaly creatures. They did not have wings, but could fly by magic.

THE DRAGON KING'S DAUGHTER

A young man named Liu was walking home when he saw a beautiful girl crying bitterly. She told him that she was the daughter of the Dragon King in human form but had married a cruel river god and moved far from home. Liu fell in love with her and promised to help her. She gave him a letter for her father and told him to go down to the lake. There, Liu was led down into the Dragon King's palace. On reading his daughter's letter, the Dragon King immediately sent an army to defeat the river god and bring her home.

After a great feast to celebrate, Liu returned home. He married a local girl but could not forget the Dragon King's daughter. When his wife died, he married again. Then a strange thing happened. His wife began to look more and more like the Dragon Princess, and soon she revealed her true identity. The two lived together happily, paying regular visits to the Dragon King's palace beneath the lake.

Dragon dances are still popular at many Chinese festivals, such as New Year celebrations.

The Dragon Boy's Pearl

There was once a poor boy who lived with his mother by a river. He earned his living by cutting grass and selling it to people to feed their animals.

One hot, dry summer, no rain fell and the soil turned to dust. The boy had to search far and wide to find any grass. By chance, he found a good, thick patch. The next day, he went back. To his surprise, the grass had grown back fresh and green, and this happened day after day. But if only it was not so far away...

"I know," the boy said, "I'll dig up a big clump and plant it at home!"

As he dug, he saw a huge, round, gleaming pearl lying in the ground. He picked it up, took it home, and gave it to his mother. While he planted the grass in his garden, she hid the pearl in a rice jar.

The next day, the grass had withered and died. But, thanks to the magic pearl, the rice jar was full. So the boy and his mother put the pearl in their money jar, and the next morning it was full of coins. They were rich!

But, one day, thieves broke into their house. Quick as a flash, the boy put the pearl in his mouth and swallowed it. At once, he felt a strange burning. He ran down to the river and began to gulp the water down. As he did so, he sprouted horns and grew scales and a long tail—he was turning into a dragon. With a mighty splash, he dived into the river, never to be seen again.

Soon afterward, the skies opened and a powerful downpour of rain fell on the parched land. The drought was over, thanks to the dragon boy's pearl.

OTHER MYTHICAL CREATURES

Apart from dragons, a huge number of fantastical creatures appear in Chinese myths. One of the most powerful was a mythical bird called the fenghuang. It was believed to nest on Mount Kunlun and only appeared very rarely, to foretell a good start to the reign of a new emperor.

FOUR SACRED ANIMALS

In Chinese mythology, the four points of the compass and the four seasons are represented by four sacred animals: the Black Tortoise of the North and winter; the Red Bird of the South and summer; the Green Dragon of the East and spring; and the White Tiger of the West and autumn.

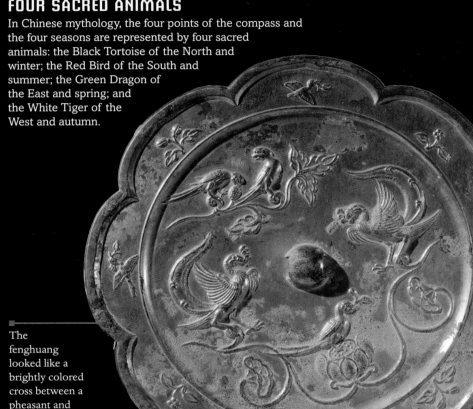

The fenghuang looked like a brightly colored cross between a pheasant and a peacock.

WHO'S WHO?

The qilin was part dragon, part deer, and part ox. It sometimes had a horn on its nose and has been compared to a unicorn. Despite its strange appearance, the qilin was a bringer of peace, prosperity, and justice. It was said to have a gentle nature, unless it saw a person being treated unfairly, when it spouted flames from its mouth.

The tortoise was a very important creature in Chinese myths. In some versions of the creation story, Pan Gu (see page 8) used a tortoise to help him keep Earth and sky apart. In another story, Nü Wa (see page 10) had to repair Earth after floods and earthquakes caused it to collapse. She caught a gigantic tortoise, cut off its four legs, and used them to prop up the four corners of Earth.

In Chinese mythology, the black tortoise stood for the north and winter.

GODS OF DAILY LIFE

The ancient Chinese had a very advanced culture. They invented paper, silk, porcelain, and gunpowder long before these items were known in the rest of the world. They had many myths about how these inventions came about, and about how the skills of daily life, such as farming and writing, were handed down to humans by gods and goddesses.

WHO'S WHO?

Shen Nong (right) taught people the secrets of farming and helped them to find new crops to grow. Legend says that he tasted all the plants himself to make sure that they were safe for humans to eat. He also invented the plow to make working the soil easier.

FU XI

The great god Fu Xi was married to Nü Wa. Like Nü Wa, he had a snake's body with a human head. According to legend, he invented fishing after watching a spider spin its web. This gave him the idea for the fishing net. Fu Xi also invented fire and China's first system of writing.

THE KITCHEN GOD

Zao Jun is also known as the Kitchen God. It was his job to make a yearly report to the Jade Emperor about the behavior of every human on Earth. When a person died, these reports were used to decide what their next life would be like. Every family had a picture of Zao Jun in their kitchen, watching over them. At New Year, the picture was burned and the smoke carried his report up to heaven. Many Chinese families still follow this tradition today.

The Kitchen God is celebrated in Vietnamese culture as well.

The Kitchen God's Wife

Long ago, Zao Jun, the Kitchen God, lived on Earth as a human being named Zhang. Zhang married a beautiful woman, Guoding, who was good, kind, and virtuous. With her help, Zhang did well in his business and soon grew important and rich. But the couple's happiness did not last long. Zhang fell in love with another woman and left his wife. The gods punished Zhang for his unfaithfulness. He lost his money and went blind. Penniless and homeless, he was forced to go begging on the streets.

One day, Zhang happened to pass the house of his first wife. Taking pity on him, Guoding took him in. Being blind, Zhang did not recognize her, but he was grateful for her kindness. Guoding saw that he looked hungry and cooked him a dish of his favorite noodles. Zhang ate them ravenously.

"These are delicious," he told her. "Just like my wife used to make."

Then he started to tell her his story, and how sorry he was for what he had done. He began to weep bitter tears.

"Open your eyes, Zhang," said Guoding gently, and at once Zhang's sight was restored.

The first thing Zhang saw when he opened his eyes was the wife whom he had abandoned long ago. But instead of being pleased, he was filled with terrible shame for the way he had treated her. In fact, he was so overcome with remorse that he threw himself into the kitchen fire, not realizing that it was lit. Desperately, Guoding tried to save him, but it was too late.

After his sad death, Zhang was made an immortal because the gods saw how sorry he was for the wrongs he had done. And so he became Zao Jun, the Kitchen God, and the gods' messenger between heaven and Earth.

THE SECRET OF SILK

The ancient Chinese were the first people to discover how to make silk from threads collected from the cocoons of silkworm moths. Chinese silk was highly prized in the West, and merchants paid huge prices for it. To safeguard their most valuable export, the Chinese kept their knowledge of silk-making a secret for thousands of years.

In ancient China, the punishment for revealing the secret of silk-making was death.

練絲
連邨煮繭香齁觧
事誰家娘盈〻
蒸媚竈拍〻手
探湯上盆頮色
好轉軸頭緒長
晚来得少休女
伴語隔墻

Many ancient Chinese characters live on in modern films. This white-haired witch appears in the 2008 film *The Forbidden Kingdom*.

LADY SILKWORM

There are several myths that explain how silk-making was discovered. In one story, a man left home on a business trip, leaving his daughter behind. She missed him so much that one day, while she was grooming her horse, she promised that she would marry anyone who brought him home. At once her horse galloped away, and soon returned with her father on its back. The girl was delighted, until she remembered her promise—the horse wanted to marry her!

Her father was horrified and killed the horse. As the girl stared sadly at its body, its skin suddenly came to life. It wrapped itself around the girl and carried her off into the sky. The next day, the girl's father saw a strange, caterpillar-like creature with a horse's head hanging in a nearby tree. It was his daughter, who had become Can Nü, or Lady Silkworm.

Did you know?

Myths live on in Chinese life today. Many people still burn a picture of the Kitchen God at New Year. New Year celebrations also include dragon dances. Myths have been retold in book, comic, and cartoon form, and characters such as the Eight Immortals have starring roles in several Chinese film and television series.

CHARACTERS, CREATURES, AND PLACES

CHARACTERS

Amituo Fu a great figure in Chinese Buddhism. He lives in a paradise, called the Pure Land, where his followers hope to go when they die.

Can Nü the silkworm goddess who was also known as Lady Silkworm

Cao Guojiu one of the eight immortals who was the brother of the earthly emperor. He turned his back on his old life and lived as a holy man.

Chang E wife of Hou Yi the archer, and goddess of the moon

Confucius philosopher and founder of Confucianism. He lived 551–479 BCE.

Faxian Chinese Buddhist monk who made a risky journey to India in 399 CE to collect Buddhist texts for translation

Fu Xi the god who brought fishing, fire, and writing to China. He was married to Nü Wa and had a snake's body with a human head.

Gun the grandson of the Yellow Emperor who helped to stop the flood that was destroying Earth

Han Xiang Zi one of the eight immortals. He studied Taoism and became a follower of Lü Dongbin.

He Xiangu one of the eight immortals and the only woman among them. She holds a lotus flower and a musical instrument called a sheng.

Hou Yi the heavenly archer who was sent to shoot down the nine suns and save Earth. He was later banished from heaven with his wife, Chang E.

Jade Emperor the ruler of heaven and the most important figure in Chinese mythology. He rules over the heavenly court of gods and goddesses.

Lan Caihe one of the eight immortals. He was famous as a healer who used medicinal plants and herbs to cure the sick.

Laozi philosopher and founder of Taoism. He probably lived during the 6th century BCE.

Li Tieguai one of the eight immortals. He is shown as an old man with an iron crutch, holding a gourd.

Lü Dongbin one of the eight immortals. He is shown dressed as a scholar, carrying a sword that makes him invisible.

Lu Wu a god with a human head, tiger's body, and nine tails who guarded Mount Kunlun, the home of the gods on Earth

Mulian a Buddhist monk who travels down to hell to save his mother from her fate as a hungry ghost

Nü Wa goddess of creation who made the first humans out of clay. She was married to Fu Xi. She had the head of a woman and the body of a snake.

Pan Gu god of creation who held Earth and sky apart. His body formed the landscapes on Earth, the weather, and the sun, moon, and stars.

Qin Shi Huang the first emperor of China, who united the country for the first time in 221 BCE and introduced standard laws and systems of money, weights, and measures

Shen Nong the god who brought farming, crops, and medicine to China. He also taught people how to use the plow.

Siddhartha Gautama an Indian nobleman who lived in the 6th century BCE and became the Buddha. The Buddhist religion is based on his teachings.

Xi Wangmu the wife of the Jade Emperor. She was also known as the Queen Mother of the West.

Yellow Emperor a great mythical emperor. He is said to have brought civilization to China.

Zao Jun also known as the Kitchen God, he was the Jade Emperor's messenger. Each year, he reported back to the emperor about how people had behaved.

Zhang Guo Lao one of the eight immortals. He lived as a holy man in the mountains and had magical powers.

Zhongli Quan one of the eight immortals. He was once an officer at the emperor's court. He holds a fan that brings the dead back to life.

CREATURES

Fenghuang mythical bird said to look like a cross between a peacock and a pheasant. It nests on Mount Kunlun.

Jian Mu a huge, mythical tree with no branches but a towering trunk. It was one of the sky ladders that linked heaven and Earth.

Monkey King (Hou Wang) a mythical creature who tricks the gods and causes mischief until the Buddha teaches him a lesson

Qilin a mythical creature that is part dragon, part deer, and part ox. It is a bringer of justice and peace.

Yu a dragon that emerged from the body of Gun and helped to stop the great flood by controlling the rivers and digging channels to lead the water away

PLACES

Duguang a paradise in the center of Earth where Jian Mu grows. It is filled with beautiful flowers and singing birds.

Mount Kunlun a sacred mountain and the home of the gods and goddesses on Earth. It was also one of the sky ladders.

Yangtze the longest river in China, which flows for about 4,039 miles (6,500 km)

Yellow the second-longest river in China (after the Yangtze), which flows for about 3,417 miles (5,500 km)

GLOSSARY

Buddhism religion that began in India in the 5th century BCE. It is based on the teachings of Siddhartha Gautama, who became the Buddha. It reached China in the 1st century CE.

civil service group of officials who carry out the day-to-day running of a country or empire

cocoons cases that butterfly and moth caterpillars build around their bodies and in which they transform into adults

Confucianism great Chinese religion based on the teachings of the wise man and philosopher Confucius, who was born in 551 BCE

court emperor and the group of people around him, including his family, minister, advisors, and servants

dynasty family who ruled China in ancient times

elixir magical liquid said to have the power to make someone immortal

enlightened having gained true knowledge and realized the true meaning of life

export object or material that is sold to other countries

gourd bottle-shaped shell of a fruit from the gourd plant

guardian someone who looks after and protects a place or person

hungry ghost ghost who was always hungry but had a very long neck, so it cannot swallow any food. People are turned into hungry ghosts as punishment for their wrongdoing.

immortal being who will live forever. The eight immortals are very important figures in Chinese mythology.

jade semiprecious stone that can be green or white. It is highly valued in China.

meditating thinking very deeply about something

mortal being who will die one day

philosopher person who is a very wise, deep-thinking teacher

porcelain clay-like material used to make plates, cups, and so on

reborn born again in another body after a person dies

righteousness living a good, responsible life; doing what is right

sacred holy or special

sheng Chinese wind instrument

silkworm caterpillar of the silk moth

sky ladder place or object, such as a tree or mountain, that acted as a link between heaven and Earth and could be used by the gods and goddesses

sobriety being sensible and not doing things to excess

social unrest time when there are problems in society, such as war or strikes

spiritual to do with religious matters or matters of the spirit or soul

supernatural magical beings and events that cannot be explained by physical or scientific laws

tablet flat piece of gold or other material that sometimes had writing on it

Taoism great Chinese religion based on the teachings of the philosopher Laozi in the 6th century BCE

virtue very good or admirable characteristic or quality

yang one of two forces that make up everything in nature, according to Taoist beliefs. Yang needs to be in balance with yin.

yin one of two forces that make up everything in nature, according to Taoist beliefs. Yin needs to be in balance with yang.

FIND OUT MORE

BOOKS

Cotterell, Arthur. *Ancient China*. New York: DK Children, 2005.

Fu, Shelley. *Treasury of Chinese Folk Tales: Beloved Myths and Legends from the Middle Kingdom*. North Clarendon, Vt.: Tuttle Publishing, 2008.

Schomp, Virginia. *The Ancient Chinese*. New York: Benchmark Books, 2009.

Van Pelt, Todd, and Rupert Matthews. *Ancient Chinese Civilization*. New York: Rosen, 2009.

Wilkinson, Philip. *Chinese Myth*. Edison, N.J.: Chartwell Books, 2007.

WEB SITES

www.ancientchina.co.uk/menu.html
The British Museum web pages on ancient China have information about geography, writing, tombs, arts, and crafts.

www.bbc.co.uk/schools/primaryhistory/worldhistory/tang_tomb_figures
These BBC web pages look at ancient China and at some of the evidence we have for its amazing culture.

www.cdot.org/history/chinese_myths.htm
This web site has a selection of Chinese myths and legends, with links to related myths in other cultures.

www.shanghaimuseum.net/en/index.jsp
The web site of the Shanghai Museum in China has a huge number of ancient Chinese artifacts to explore.

PLACES TO VISIT

The Metropolitan Museum of Art
New York, New York
www.metmuseum.org
The Met has a section devoted to Asian art, with a rotating collection.

Freer/Sackler (The Smithsonian's Museums of Asian Art)
Washington, DC
www.asia.si.edu
These galleries of the Smithsonian Institution include a collection of Chinese jades and bronzes.

The Los Angeles County Museum of Art
Los Angeles, California
www.lacma.org
The LACMA has a collection of Chinese art ranging from ancient to modern artworks.

National Museum of China
Beijing, China
http://en.chnmuseum.cn
China's huge National Museum has artifacts from ancient China and more modern times.

FURTHER RESEARCH

Which Chinese myth did you like reading most in this book? Which characters did you find most interesting? Can you find out about any more myths in which these characters appear? You could look in the books or on the web sites given here, or even visit some of the places mentioned. You could also try retelling your favorite myth in a new way, such as a diary, a cartoon strip, or a newspaper report.

INDEX